# SAVED FOR THE PEOPLE OF PENNSYLVANIA

Quilts from *The State Museum of Pennsylvania*

*Lucinda Reddington Cawley*

*Lorraine DeAngelis Ezbiansky*

*Denise Rocheleau Nordberg*

Commonwealth of Pennsylvania

Pennsylvania Historical and Museum Commission

Harrisburg, 1997

© 1997
Commonwealth of Pennsylvania
ISBN O - 89271 - 073 - X

WHITEWORK WITH
SASHING (detail)
Maker unknown
Circa 1850
104"x102"
Catalogue 40.43.2

*This detail shows one of the many intricate quilting motifs that grace this mid-nineteenth century piece. Quilts such as this, which have large open spaces featuring different designs, are known as quilting samplers, and were popular until the end of the Civil War.[1] This example contains over twenty elaborate, stuffed, finely stitched designs. Other details of this quilt may be found on pages 5 and 6.*

*Front cover:*
STAR OF BETHLEHEM (detail)
Catalogue 31.96.17
*Detail from Sally Albright's quilt, found with a description on page 58.*

*Back cover:*
DOUBLE IRISH CHAIN
Circa 1900
88"x83.5"
Catalogue 64.56.48
*The unknown maker of this quilt chose an unusual color combination that adds distinction to a common pattern.*

## CHAPTER 1

The State Museum of Pennsylvania, located in Harrisburg and administered by the Pennsylvania Historical and Museum Commission, collects and preserves objects associated with Pennsylvania's history and heritage and interprets this heritage through exhibits and public programs. Since its founding in 1905, The State Museum has collected approximately 1.9 million objects spanning Pennsylvania paleontology, geology, natural science, archaeology, fine arts, military, political and industrial history, and community and domestic life. The State Museum exhibits a small percentage of these objects to educate visitors about the Commonwealth's past. The remainder are in the care of museum curators, preserved for future display and available to staff and public for research and study.

Pennsylvania quilts are an important part of The State Museum's varied collections. Since 1924 the museum has acquired almost two hundred of them, making this the largest collection in the Commonwealth. The collection grew slowly at first. For many years quilts were little appreciated for their magnificent artistry and historical significance. Donations and purchases of quilts trickled into The State Museum from the first gift in 1924 and continued through the 1950s. During the 1960s and 1970s, however, Americans gained a greater appreciation of their folk traditions, including quiltmaking. Awakened to the beauty and significance of quilts and spurred by the nation's observance of its bicentennial, Pennsylvanians during two decades donated over one hundred quilts in many different styles. For their part, curators with their own deepening appreciation expanded the depth and breadth of the collection. The State Museum's collection now preserves Pennsylvania's quiltmaking heritage for all of us to learn from and enjoy.

The museum's quilts are visually exciting works of folk art, with bold colors and designs that demand attention. Interestingly enough, these quilts usually do not see the light of day; they are stored in darkness away from the light which can quickly fade their colors and damage their cloth. State Museum staff occasionally bring quilts out of storage for inspection, cleaning or conservation, and, on rare occasions, exhibition. Because museum staff cannot exhibit the quilts for long periods without damaging them, The State Museum, the Pennsylvania Historical and Museum Commission, and the Friends of The State Museum (the non-profit supporting affiliate of The State Museum) have sponsored this publication as a way for those interested to learn more about them. This book offers a visual sampling of the quilts and an overview of the many styles found in the collection.

The State Museum also undertakes the conservation and repair of quilts that have come to the collection in deteriorated condition. The museum has limited funding to accomplish this important and expensive work of conservation. To help preserve these quilts for future generations, the Friends of The State Museum have created a fund dedicated to their conservation and repair. If you would like to help, you are invited to make a contribution to the Friends of The State Museum, earmarked for "The State Museum Quilt Preservation Fund." To contribute or learn more about this fund, please contact the Friends of The State Museum at P.O. Box 1026, Harrisburg, Pennsylvania 17108-1026.

William Sisson
Chief, Curatorial Division
The State Museum of Pennsylvania

We would like to take this opportunity to thank those who have helped us make this book a reality.

Anita Blackaby, Director, The State Museum of Pennsylvania, provided the necessary support and resources of the museum to bring this project to fruition.

The curators and staff of the museum have worked diligently to acquire and maintain this outstanding collection; it is because of their efforts that we have these quilts to share with you. William Sisson, Chief, Curatorial Division, initiated both the documentation project and the book, and Mary Jane Hayward, Registrar, worked with us on the documentation, locating materials and helping us find answers. Beatrice Hulsberg in the Community and Domestic Life Section provided curatorial assistance. Diane Reed, Chief, Division of Publications of the Pennsylvania

WHITEWORK WITH
SASHING (detail)
Circa 1850
104" x 102"
Catalogue 40.43.2

Historical and Museum Commission, has been an enthusiastic and knowledgeable publisher. Kimberly Krammes, the designer, and Claire Messimer, the photographer, combined their artistic talents to make this book beautiful.

Information for a work like this is not found in only one place; consequently, we have been on the road and on the phone for months, gathering insights and background. Patricia T. Herr, Mary H. Robinson, and Brian R. Katchur have been generous and helpful to us in our project. Our research has benefitted from the resources of the York County Historical Society, the Pioneer Historical Society of Bedford County, the Dimmick Memorial Library of Jim Thorpe, the Lehigh County Historical Society, the Wyoming Historical and Geological Society of Wilkes-Barre, Linden Hall School for Girls in Lititz, and the library of the Church of Jesus Christ of Latter Day Saints in Clarks Summit.

Dorothy Reddington, Cultural Advisor to Governor Robert P. Casey, introduced us to the quilt collection at The State Museum, and thus set us on the path to this book.

Cheryl Starr Hayward volunteered to be our helper and became our scribe, our lunchmate, the fourth member of our documentation team, and our friend.

We are grateful to our families for the love and support which enabled us to undertake and complete this project.

When The State Museum of Pennsylvania acquired Sally Albright's Star of Bethlehem quilt (see page 58), there was a note attached to the back which said, "Save for the people of Pennsylvania." The museum's collection of quilts and related textiles is the result of the generosity of donors and the farsightedness of curators who shared her sentiment. Begun in 1924 with the accession of a pair of pieced pillowcases, the collection now includes almost two hundred pieces with many styles and techniques of American quiltmaking represented. The earliest quilts date from about 1800 while the most recent are those made to celebrate the Bicentennial of the Declaration of Independence in 1976. Since quiltmaking is such an important Pennsylvania craft, it is fitting that there are many quilts which reveal a particularly Pennsylvanian sensibility. Another strength of the collection is the number and variety of crazy quilts.

A documentation of the quilt collection was completed in 1995. A form developed for this project was used to record physical details about each item in the collection. Information was gathered from museum files, census and genealogical records and local historical societies. The documentation forms, including slides and photographs of each item, are available for study.

This book was written in order to share the beauties of the collection with the widest possible audience.

The highlights of the collection are arranged into six broad categories. The first category includes early quilts which show the evolution from the English needlework tradition to the distinctly American repeat-block style.[2] The signature-quilt category includes examples from the mid-nineteenth century whose documentations are more complete because research has unlocked some of their mysteries. The next chapter features classic red and green appliqué quilts which were popular everywhere in America between 1840 and 1870. Pieced quilts, representing a century of American quiltmaking, form the largest category. Examples in this section range from the simplest block designs to the most intricate stars. The silk quilt chapter which follows includes an early one-patch, a commemorative ribbon quilt, and classic crazy quilts. The quilts in the final category are quintessentially Pennsylvanian in style or color, illustrating the primary position of Pennsylvania in the evolution of American quiltmaking.

Each chapter includes an introduction which explores the social context of the quilts and their place in the history of American quiltmaking. After each introduction, masterpiece and representative quilts are pictured and described. A photograph illustrates each quilt with accompanying information on the commonly accepted pattern name, the size (height first), the approximate date, the museum catalogue number, and whenever known, the place where the quilt was made and the name of its maker. (Since all of the quiltmakers who have been identified are women, feminine pronouns are used throughout.) Following the text are a glossary, a bibliography and a complete list of the collection by catalogue number.

WHITEWORK WITH
SASHING (detail)
Circa 1850
104" x 102"
Catalogue 40.43.2

# EARLY QUILTS

Women from the British Isles have long been known for their needle skills and many outstanding examples of their quilted bedcovers have survived. The first women to immigrate to the English colonies in America were trained in this tradition; however, few quilts were made during the early colonial period because the necessary materials and time were not available. Once the survival of the community was assured, women were able to use their needles creatively and quilted bedcoverings in the European tradition appeared. The primary impetus for quiltmaking has always been the urge to create something beautiful as well as useful. While quilts were made for practical purposes, those very early quilts that have survived are usually a showcase for the skills of the maker.

During the eighteenth and early nineteenth century all fabric made in America was hand woven. Textiles were scarce and expensive. Fabric imported from Europe influenced the aesthetic sensibility of American women and American quilts mirrored their English counterparts. The earliest examples of American quilts are almost always one of three styles seen in quilts made in England during the same period: whole-cloth, medallion and one-patch.[3] With the beginning of factory production of fabric in the United States in the mid 1820s, an enormous quantity and variety of high quality, inexpensive printed cottons became available and an explosion of productivity by American quiltmakers resulted.

While early appliqué was usually an attempt to stretch expensive imported chintzes, the increased availability of fabric allowed American women to experiment. A freer, less formal American style of appliqué resulted. The enormous variety of block designs did not develop gradually but burst into American quiltmaking; by 1850 sampler, album, repeat-block, four-block and nine-block quilts had all appeared.

The following examples from the collection of The State Museum of Pennsylvania have been chosen to illustrate the styles of quiltmaking popular from 1800 to 1850. One is a simple pieced baby quilt; the others represent the pinnacle of the quiltmaker's art.

*The finely quilted scrap Nine-Patch on the following page was made for Amos Kapp by his nurse, Kitty Dupes, when he was born in 1809. Amos became an influential businessman and community leader in the Borough of Northumberland, running packet boats and coaches along the Susquehanna River. It is said that he attended twenty-two Pennsylvania gubernatorial inaugurations in his lifetime, and that one of his coaches was the last such conveyance to carry a Pennsylvania governor to his swearing-in ceremony.*

*The hexagon quilt on page 9, which uses some of the same fabrics as Amos's quilt, was made by his sister Catharine in 1814. Catharine had been a boarding student at the Moravian Girls' School (now called Linden Hall) in Lititz, Pennsylvania. Founded in 1746, it is one of the oldest girls' schools in the United States. The Moravians believed that female education was essential to the well-being of the community.[4] In addition to reading, writing, grammar, arithmetic, history and geography, the girls learned needlework.[5] One of Catharine's embroideries is still on display at the school. She must also have been influenced by her mother, Mary Elmaker Kapp, whose exceptional stuffed work can be seen in three dresser scarves in The State Museum's collection. In this quilt Catharine used fine fabrics and a brilliant yellow pillar print to create an elegant showcase for her needle skills. She then cross-stitched her name and the date in one of the hexagons. Catharine, who never married, returned to Harrisburg after leaving Lititz and lived in the family home until her death in 1880.*

*These two quilts came to the museum separately. Amos's was donated by his daughter Helen in 1929, and Catharine's was purchased from a non-family member in 1931. It is unlikely that the relationship between the quilts was known at that time, because there is no mention of it in the museum records. The Kapp name and the shared fabric found in the quilts during this documentation led to the discovery of the family connection.*

AMOS KAPP'S CRADLE QUILT
Kitty Dupes
1809
Harrisburg, Dauphin County
37"x29"
Catalogue 29.30.5

HEXAGON QUILT
Catharine Kapp (1799-1880)
1814
Harrisburg, Dauphin County
120"x97"
Catalogue 31.63.6

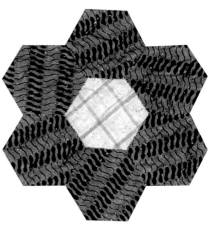

*This detail and the one
on the previous page
show the fabric shared by
the two Kapp quilts.*

FEATHERED STAR
Maker unknown
1825-1850
106"x103"
Catalogue 83.58

*This quilt is described on
the following page.*

*Fine piecework and exceptional quilting highlight the lovely Feathered Star on the opposite page. Made in the second quarter of the nineteenth century, it is accompanied by a ribbon from the 1893 Chicago Columbian Exposition which reads "Oldest Quilt" and "Most Distinctive Quilting." Stuffed grape clusters and feathered wreaths fill the open blocks, and some of the background is stippled.*

*This quilt is a "star" in more ways than one. The center of its medallion set is a variable star, and the ten borders surrounding it are a "stellar" collection of early prints, pieced with an artist's eye and a draftsman's skill. This artist/draftsman's name was "N. Virginia Robinson Drum." She had the foresight to add her name and the inscription "June 16th, 1800 Pittsburg, Pa" to the back of her masterpiece as shown in the detail above.*

MEDALLION QUILT
N. Virginia Robinson Drum
1800
Pittsburgh, Allegheny County
93"x81"
Catalogue 70.50.8

*This spectacular medallion quilt, unlike most of its contemporaries, uses only one print fabric, a glazed navy chintz with green dots. The blue and white combination and the quiltmaker's exceptional use of positive and negative images give this quilt a bolder, more graphic sensibility than other medallions of the time. Also, the high-contrast color scheme emphasizes the precision with which this quilt was drafted and pieced. Signed "Alice Cochran" in the quilting, it is a work of art. The large stain in the center was probably caused by water damage while it was folded and stored; otherwise the quilt is in pristine condition.*

CHINTZ MEDALLION
Alice Cochran
1825-1850
108"x106"
Catalogue 44.27

(detail)
Catalogue 44.27

*This detail of Alice Cochran's quilt shows the skillful way in which she repeated the sunburst corner motif in each of her borders, using alternately dark and light images and enlarging the design to fit the scale of each border. Note the heavy glaze that is still apparent on the blue fabric.*

This outstanding stuffed whitework quilt is one of the treasures of the collection. The original quilting motifs of baskets, melons, vines, grapes and leaves are well placed, finely stuffed, and carefully executed. Surrounding the designs is background quilting in diagonal rows one-eighth inch apart, done in small stitches (thirteen to the inch).

Elaborate quilts such as this were often made by young women in anticipation of marriage. Hannah Welsh, the maker of this piece, was born in York County and married Dr. Obediah Dingee of Lancaster County in 1823. Both the date of the quilt provided by family members and the quality of the workmanship indicate that this was probably Hannah's wedding quilt. The quilt remained in Hannah's family until 1972, when it was damaged in the Agnes Flood and then donated to the museum after professional conservation. Other details from this quilt appear on pages 59, 64, and 66.

WHITEWORK QUILT (details)
Hannah Welsh (1798-?)
Circa 1820
York, York County
108"x106"
Catalogue 81.10

This lovely broderie perse medallion is a summer spread; that is, it is backed but has no batting or quilting. It contains an extensive collection of early printed fabrics. An interesting zigzag border, which appears frequently among the older quilts in this collection, is used here to define the center and outermost edges of the quilt.

BRODERIE PERSE SUMMER SPREAD
Jane Griffith Roberts
Circa 1828
Harrisburg, Dauphin County
83"x72"
Catalogue 79.99.1

Friendship, album and signature quilts, the fabric equivalent of the autograph album fad of the second quarter of the nineteenth century, began to appear around 1840 among the Quakers in the Delaware Valley of southeastern Pennsylvania.[6] By that time, the earlier medallion-style quilts had been replaced in popularity by the repeat-block designs which offered quiltmakers the opportunity to look at their quilts as a collection of pages. From the beginning, friendship quilts were made in various styles, ranging from the simple, repeated, pieced block to the elaborate appliqué of Baltimore album quilts.

Album quilts differ from other quilts not in their physical characteristics but in their purpose, which is not warmth but memory. No quilt is ever deliberately made for the short term, but more than any others, signature quilts are intended to be heirlooms. Whether as a tangible reminder of those left behind in the westward migration, a celebration of weddings or births, an expression of group identity, or a means to raise funds for an important cause, these quilts are made to connect the past to the future.

During and after the Civil War, signature quilts became a popular and reliable fund-raising device. For a small fee, one's name could be included on a quilt representing the members of a specific community, perhaps a church or fraternal organization. The quilt might then be raffled or auctioned to raise money for a common cause.

By the end of the nineteenth century, the most popular album-style quilts were variations of the red and white embroideries made from preprinted blocks called penny squares. Originality of design returned with the great quilt revival of the 1920s and 1930s.

Probably more album quilts are being made today than ever before. The most striking example of the revived interest in signature quilts is the Names Project, the enormous quilt composed of blocks created in memory of those who have died of AIDS. Today, as in the 1840s, the names, dates and places recorded on a quilt inspire an interest in its maker and his or her community, and open avenues of research for future generations.

The collection of The State Museum contains examples of all kinds of signature quilts except those made specifically as fund-raisers. There is a red and white penny-square quilt and a Bicentennial quilt signed by Governor Shapp and President and Mrs. Ford. All but one of the quilts illustrated date from around 1850.

# SIGNATURE QUILTS

*The quilt on the following page was presented to the Reverend Dr. John F. Mesick, pastor of the Salem German Reformed Church from 1840 to 1855, by his congregation. The Peony is a classic applique design and it is not unusual that it was chosen to honor a beloved pastor. There are thirty-six names on the applique squares and all but four are legible. These names were compared with church records of the period and identified as those of members of the congregation. After his time as pastor in Harrisburg, the Reverend Dr. Mesick served as vice president of Franklin and Marshall College. The quilt descended to Dr. Mesick's daughter Anna Mesick Gross and was donated to the museum by one of her granddaughters.*

PEONY
Ladies of the Salem
German Reformed Church
1847
Harrisburg,
Dauphin County
93"x91"
Catalogue 76.65

LEMOYNE STAR
Maker unknown
1850-1860
96"x105"
Catalogue 31.96.15

*This LeMoyne Star signature quilt uses many mid-nineteenth century red print fabrics in its stars. The zigzag sashing creates a graphic impact uncommon in most variations of this pattern. The innovative maker of this piece cut away the centers of the stars, thus removing a difficult and often bulky juncture and leaving instead a convenient place for signatures.*

*This quilt is a puzzle. When The State Museum purchased it in 1931 it came with information that read, "From Esther Morrison, b. 1836. Made by her mother before Esther was married," but the initials "J.A." are embroidered in a corner of the top, and one cryptic signature reads "Ruth Ann Parry, Proprietor."*

*Although many of the fifty-four signatures are accompanied by place names (most commonly Bucks and Lancaster Counties and Philadelphia), there are no dates. The signers who have been found in records (family names Parry, Stubbs and Brosius) belong to the Society of Friends, which is not surprising, since signature quilts were popularized by the Quakers. Because no other common thread has been found, the quilt's significance and its maker are lost to history.*

Euphemia Reese Wilson was born in Moreland, Pennsylvania, near Philadelphia, in 1790. In 1814, she married John Righter Jr. and moved to Beaver Meadow where her father, William H. Wilson, a Revolutionary War hero, was the first known resident.[7] In 1820, when her husband John died, she had three small children, Jane, W.W., and John W.

When she signed the large center Double Compass square of her quilt "Mrs. Euphemia Righter, Beaver Meadow, Penna, February 8th, 1850," Euphemia was listed in the census as the head of a household of more than a dozen unrelated people; she probably was running a boarding house. Her son John was living next door to her with his wife Margaretta and her son W.W. Righter was a physician in Berwick. Her daughter Jane's strong signature on the quilt has "Americus, Georgia" added to it. Although no significance has been attached to the date in the center square, the dates on all of the other smaller squares predate it, ranging from January 1844 to February 1850, and seem to be grouped by family names.

The signatures on the quilt have not all been identified but those that have are a mixture of relatives and community members. Daughters-in-law Margaretta and Jane signed the quilt, as did several men who had served on the school board with her son John. Other signers of the quilt include patients of Euphemia's son W.W. and Mrs. Anna Von Tagen, the wife of the local mine owner.

The center Double Compass is a very difficult design and this example is beautifully sewn; the points are sharp and the center lies flat. The thirty-two smaller blocks are a simpler compass design. The techniques used indicate that one person made all of the blocks, although each block has been signed individually.

Euphemia signed the center square of this beautifully made and preserved quilt to link her name with those of her friends and family. Almost 150 years later, we are reminded of them in relation to Euphemia, who has given us a glimpse into her life and the community in which she stays forever centered.

(detail) center block
Catalogue 83.69

MARINER'S COMPASS
AUTOGRAPH QUILT
Euphemia Reese Wilson
Righter (1790-1873)
1850
Beaver Meadow,
Carbon County
111"x108"
Catalogue 83.69

APPLIQUÉ ALBUM QUILT
Probably Rebecca Garretson
Wickersham (1791-1873)
Circa 1854
Newberry Township,
York County
107"x 99"
Catalogue 65.78

The inscription on the center block of this beautiful quilt reads "John Wickersham was born 24 Dec. 1780 died 22 Feb 1853." Next to it is a block which says, "Rebecca Wickersham was born the 6th day of the 3rd month 1791." It is likely that Rebecca made the quilt as a memorial to her husband. Of the fifty-seven signers of the quilt thirty-nine have been identified; all of them resided in northern York County in 1850 and most were related to the Wickershams.

As indicated by the style of the date in Rebecca's block, the Wickershams were Quakers. The family settled in Pennsylvania in the days of William Penn and were among the founders of the Warrenton Meeting in York County in 1745. Other names found on the quilt, for example Kirk and Garretson, were also associated with the Society of Friends.

In 1851 Thomas Wickersham, a nephew of John and Rebecca, emigrated with his family to Iowa. His daughter Eliza Mary received quilt blocks as parting gifts from her friends in York County. The summer spread made from these blocks, now in a private collection in Kansas, bears a remarkable resemblance to Rebecca's album quilt. Five names appear on both quilts.[8]

This splendid quilt, in which each block is a different design, is a Pennsylvania interpretation of the Baltimore Album appliqué style popular between 1845 and 1855. The influence of Baltimore is unmistakable, but there are many differences. The overall design is freer and less formal than in Baltimore quilts and the ten-and-one-half-inch blocks are smaller. The appliqué motifs are clearly derived from the Pennsylvania German folk idiom. Most Baltimore appliqué designs are more complex than the single, relatively large elements found on these blocks. Unlike the subtle gradation of color often found on Baltimore quilts, the overall effect of this quilt is high contrast with a more liberal use of yellow and orange. Most of the motifs are embellished with buttonhole stitch, a characteristic of York County appliqué.[9]

Not all the blocks are signed by the same hand and variations in workmanship indicate that they were stitched by a number of people, but it is obvious that this group effort was carefully planned and well organized. The partial blocks, which fill the edges of the quilt with a heart-shaped motif, all appear to have been made by the same person. It is elegantly quilted with twelve stitches to the inch.

APPLIQUÉ ALBUM QUILT
(detail)
Catalogue 65.78

*John Wickersham's birth and death are recorded in the center of this block.*

FRIENDSHIP QUILT
Caroline Brobst (1837-1879)
1852
Lynn Township, Lehigh County
86"x 86"
Catalogue 68.78

(detail)
Catalogue 68.78

twenties. Some were cousins of Caroline or members of her 1851 confirmation class at the Jerusalem Church, Albany Township, Berks County. Variations in the stitching indicate that the quilting was done by more than one person; perhaps some of the girls who signed the quilt helped their friend Caroline to finish it.

Caroline married Franklin Camp sometime in the late 1850s. They had five children before her death at age forty-one. She is buried in Lynn Township, where she lived all her life. This quilt, beautifully preserved, is her memorial.

The maker of this fine example of a Pennsylvania German friendship quilt, pieced in the Rolling Stone design, left no doubt about her identity. It is signed, in ornately decorated calligraphy, "Caroline Brobst, In Lynn Township, Lehigh County, 1852." When she made the quilt Caroline was a fifteen-year-old orphan living in the farm home of John and Catharine Reinhart.

There are twenty-eight names elaborately inked by the same hand. All of those which have been identified are of young people in their teens or early

Elizabeth Shriver was identified as the maker of the unfinished friendship quilt on the next page by researching the family relationships recorded on the papers pinned to the blocks. Seventeen of the twenty-four lily blocks have a paper attached recording a name, a date ranging from October 15 to 30, 1879, and usually an indication of the person's relationship to the maker of the quilt or a sentiment of friendship. The spelling and punctuation are unconventional. Arther[sic] Imler's block says "From my sister her youngest son good bye dear ant." Mollie Imler's block refers to her only sister. William Reininger's says, "This is from my brother." Mary O. Imler identifies herself as a member of the Lutheran Church at Barley. The blocks were made by different people and the inscriptions are in several hands.

All the signers are members of the family of Elizabeth Reininger, the grandmother of the maker *of the quilt top, who lived in Woodbury Township, Bedford County, from 1784 to 1879. The quilt top dates from the year of her death and may have been started when the family gathered for her funeral. Elizabeth Shriver seems to have been the only member of the family to leave the Woodbury area. When she married in 1870, she moved to Fulton County; this quilt may have been intended to be a reminder of the relatives she left behind.*

LILY FRIENDSHIP QUILT TOP
Elizabeth Reininger Shriver
(1839-?)
Circa 1879
Bedford or Fulton County
82"x58"
Catalogue 34.38

(detail)
Catalogue 34.38

*This scrap of paper, one of seventeen sewn to the quilt top, reads "Oc the 20 1879. Mollie A. Imler present this pash to her onley sister wen this you see o think of me you ar far away."*

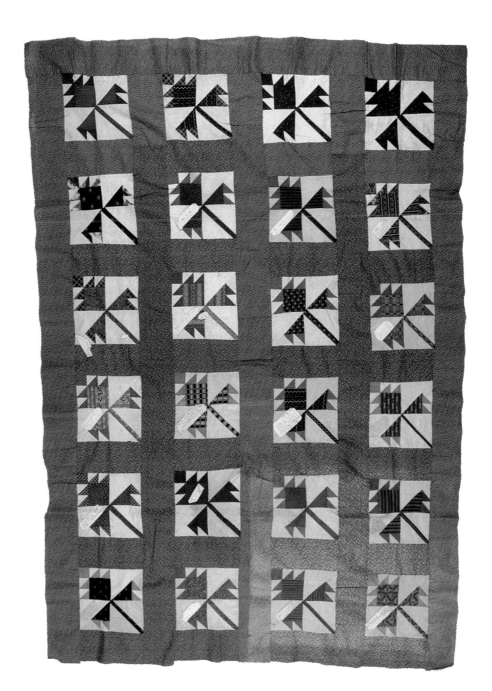

# CLASSIC RED AND GREEN APPLIQUÉ QUILTS 1840-1870

In every settled state, and especially in Pennsylvania, the years between 1840 and 1870 saw a flowering of quilts made primarily in red and green. The classic quilt of this period was a repeat-block floral appliqué design on a background of white or off-white fabric with a related border and beautiful quilting. Many of these quilts survive and are documented because they were made for best, brought out only on special occasions, and preserved by succeeding generations.

Some generalizations can be made about red and green appliqué quilts. Most of these quilts required fine sewing skills and the time to finish them. Since the amount of time needed to make an appliqué quilt is considerable, most were sewn by women either before marriage or after their children were grown.[10] These quilts were also both an indulgence and a status symbol. The maker had to be free from the rigors of frontier living and able to afford the fabric.

Although most of the classic red and green quilts follow a well-established formula of pattern, design and color, there were regional differences as distinctive as the Baltimore Album quilts and

the vivid background colors of some made in Pennsylvania. Baltimore Albums were made by upper-middle-class women who used expensive imported fabrics to fashion quilts made from blocks of different styles. The Laurel Leaf and President's Wreath, which were more commonly used as repeat-blocks in other sections of the country, were often included as a single block in the album quilts; while the most sophisticated blocks were made of baskets, bouquets and wreaths of three-dimensional, realistic flowers. In Pennsylvania, as in the rest of the country, repeat-block appliqué patterns were favored and the flowers were based on the two-dimensional German folk designs seen on blanket chests, fractur, painted theorems, and scherenschnitte (papercut designs). Four-block quilts were also primarily a Pennsylvania interpretation of the classic appliqué style.[11]

The tremendous popularity of this quilt style and color combination is, according to quilt historians, a result of a number of factors. Women had been seeing similar designs and colors in

previous decades but only the wealthy could afford the expensive imported fabrics needed to make quilts. By 1840 the flourishing domestic fabric industry was producing a "turkey red" fabric which used a colorfast dye process. Also available was an aniline green which was known to fade to an acceptable shade. Reliable dyes were essential because no one would make such a time-consuming quilt only to have it bleed or fade. Although these red and green fabrics were relatively expensive, much smaller quantities were needed than of the background fabric, which cost far less. The availability and reasonable price of these fabrics meant that women of more modest means, both urban and rural, could mimic the broderie perse quilts made by the wealthy at the beginning of the century.[12]

In addition to the availability of the raw materials needed for these classic quilts, their popularity spread quickly thanks to the system of roads, canals and railroads connecting urban and rural communities. The classic red and green appliqué quilt appeared first in the East, and the greatest concentrations have been found in the German communities of Pennsylvania and Ohio.[13] In quilt documentations done in the Plains States, a pattern of migration has been established which usually begins in Pennsylvania.[14] Red and green appliqué quilts were sent with settlers to remind them of their connections and to give them something beautiful and sophisticated even in the midst of hardship.[15]

As much as women of the period wanted to own one of these classic quilts, they also wanted to have something unique. Even when copying a pattern for a block taken from a quilt at the fair, or using a neighbor's border design, each maker would inject some of her own sensibility. The museum is fortunate to have a sampling of quilts from the era of classic red and green appliqué exhibiting the unique elements brought to that tradition by each quiltmaker.

CAROLINA LILY QUILT (detail)
Maker unknown
Circa 1850
106" x 104"
Catalogue 60.55.1

*The detail above illustrates the intricate quilting that was a feature of the red and green quilts from 1840 -1870.*

CAROLINA LILY QUILT
Maker unknown
Circa 1850
106" x 104"
Catalogue 60.55.1

*Nothing is known about the maker of this superb quilt except that the initials "W.M." are signed in ink. Although the Carolina Lily is a very common repeat block pattern, the beautiful stuffed wreaths ornamenting the plain blocks make this an outstanding example of the classic red and green period.*

CACTUS [16]
Elizabeth Smith (1823-1889)
Circa 1860
Newport, Perry County
85"x85"
Catalogue 61.54.6

*Four-block quilts were very popular during the red and green appliqué period and most were made in Pennsylvania around 1860. Although this quilt is well within the classic red and green appliqué tradition, the Cactus design is very unusual. Two similar examples were identified in the Berks County Quilt Harvest project[17] and are in a private collection. Another Cactus quilt, found in Sullivan County, looks very different because of its set.[18] The border of Elizabeth Smith's quilt, which was probably an original design, is primitive in contrast with the intricate center blocks.*

*The quilt on the opposite page, called the Brown Family Quilt by the donor, is a fine example of the classic red and green appliqué style made in a nine-block set. The addition of chrome yellow and pink enhances its beauty. As traditional as the Whig Rose pattern is, the border design on this quilt is unique. Reverse appliqué leaves balanced by a flower spray have as their fulcrum an unusual red mask-like shape. The design flows and is well balanced. The quilting is fine and elaborate with an all-over grid design and feather motifs circling the Whig Rose pattern and framing the border designs.*

WHIG ROSE
Maker unknown
Circa 1850
96"x96"
Catalogue SH65.1

LAUREL LEAF
Sabina Oberly (1822-1906)
1847
Northampton County
104"x104"
Catalogue 76.94

*In this quilt the Laurel Leaf pattern is used to sash quilted blocks rather than as the primary design element. (See detail on the opposite page.) With all the color in the sashing, this set is meant to frame large intricately quilted squares. A balance between the quilting and the appliqué has been achieved by using a common pattern in an uncommon way. Sabina Oberly made the quilt in 1847 before her marriage to William Sandt.*

LAUREL LEAF (detail)
Maker unknown
Circa 1850
95" x 93"
Catalogue 76.169.1

The Laurel Leaf was one of the most popular patterns of the red and green period; most, such as this one, were made as repeat-block designs. This variation blunts the green leaves and transforms the block so that it frames the alternating plain blocks which are beautifully quilted with circular feathers, grids, chevrons and pumpkin seeds. This detail is included to show the more common set of a Laurel Leaf quilt.

TULIPS AND BERRIES
Maker unknown
Circa 1850
96"x86"
Catalogue 70.50.9

*This classic red and green appliqué quilt is an unusual design. In each block there are three berries near the corners, between two triple-leaf motifs. The border features vases of tulips with the same triple berries and leaves. The use of one red and one green fabric throughout unites the center with its border. Although the quilting is close and the stitches are fine, the lovely appliqué design is what makes this quilt so attractive.*

# PIECED QUILTS

The pieced quilt is what most people think of when they hear the word "quilt," calling to mind a bright log cabin or a simple nine-patch. Repeat-block design was the major stylistic innovation of American quilts. Most pieced quilts were made in basic, easily constructed patterns which offered the maker an opportunity to display the richness of her scrap bag. These quilts were intended to provide bedcoverings for the family and most were worn out in the course of daily life. However, many quiltmakers challenged themselves to work with designs of enormous complexity such as Mariner's Compass. The maker was very likely to take special pains to preserve those quilts which tested her skill with the needle.

The impact of a pieced quilt does not always depend on the technical difficulty of its construction. Some very simple quilts, pieced only of squares, charm by their interesting scale or joyous use of color. The plain setting blocks and wide borders often found on pieced quilts allow the maker to display her quilting skills. Feathered wreaths, vines and flowers, sometimes embellished with stuffed work, can transform a simple pieced quilt into a showpiece. Stars in endless variations have been the most popular quilt designs.[19] There are simple Ohio Star and LeMoyne Star blocks which allow for creativity in color and set.

NINE PATCH (detail)
Landis-Piper Family
1878-1900
Cumberland County
90"x75"
Catalogue 72.190.2

*The individual squares in this quilt measure only seven-eighths of an inch. The Nine Patch, one of the most popular of all quilt patterns, is seldom made of such small pieces.*

The glorious Lone Star quilts challenge the accomplished seamstress to make hundreds of diamond-shaped pieces fit together perfectly. The Feathered Star is the ultimate test of the piecer's skill.

Printed sources for quilt patterns were not widely available before the late nineteenth century. Until that time most people probably learned about new quilt patterns from friends and relatives and by attending fairs and exhibitions where needlework was displayed. Popular designs spread rapidly through these informal networks. Quiltmakers often made a collection of sample blocks never intended to be part of a finished quilt.[20]

STAR OF BETHLEHEM MEDALLION (detail)
Catalogue 80.42
(See page 50.)

By 1883 *Farm and Fireside* was regularly publishing patterns for quilt blocks. The Ladies Art Company, founded in 1889, offered patterns by mail order.[21] Commercialization led to the proliferation of names for quilt patterns. Early quiltmakers were far less concerned with assigning a specific name to their quilts than quilters are today. The enormous variety of patterns is probably the result of each quilter expressing her individual taste and skill through her work.

The collection of The State Museum of Pennsylvania includes examples of everyday pieced quilts as well as masterpieces. It contains quilts made in the early nineteenth century, several which mark the celebration of the Bicentennial in 1976, and fine examples of the changing tastes of America's quiltmakers through the intervening years.

STAR VARIATION (detail)
Maker unknown
1850-1900
Catalogue SH70.352

*This star variation is an unusual and challenging pattern. It is pieced in indigo blue and white.*

VARIABLE STAR (detail)
Maker unknown
Circa 1880
Catalogue 76.169.2

*Sometimes called Ohio Star, this block is a great favorite with quiltmakers; it is relatively easy to piece and can be set together in many different ways.*

BIRDS IN FLIGHT BABY QUILT
Catherine Gudila Burgaman Swengel (1832-1872)
Circa 1850
41"x31"
Catalogue 65.38.1

*Since baby quilts were usually worn out by hard use, scarcity adds interest to those which remain. Nineteenth-century quilts for children were usually smaller versions of the patterns used for bed quilts; designs with nursery themes and pastel colors did not become popular until the 1920s. The restrained color scheme of this quilt is enhanced by elaborate quilting. The triangle border along two sides may mean that it was made for a crib that stood against a wall, or it may have been a choice made to balance the overall design. Another of Catherine Swengel's quilts is pictured on page 52.*

LILY
Maker unknown
1880-1910
72"x70"
Catalogue 64.55.1

*Beauty was important to quilters even in the construction of everyday quilts. While each of the pieced blocks in this quilt is identical, the maker demonstrated the effects that can be achieved by varying color and fabric. This quilt was made to be used; it has simple utility quilting. However, in spite of much wear, it remains a beautiful example of the possibilities of repeat-block design.*

*The interesting Depression-era quilt on the facing page is similar to the popular Dresden Plate design. Instead of being appliquéd to a plain background, the hexagons are pieced together with the colors arranged to form a series of interlocking stars. The color and fabrics are unmistakably from the 1930s, a period when quiltmaking was enjoying an enthusiastic revival. The Nile green in the border is a signature color of the period.*

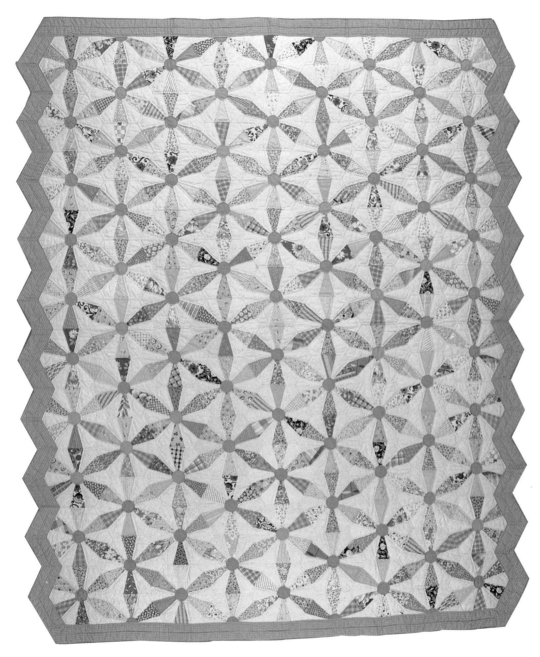

ENDLESS CHAIN [22]
Maker unknown
Circa 1930
81" x 68"
Catalogue 73.220

ROOSEVELT-LANDON QUILT (detail)
Maker unknown
Circa 1936
Bradford County
84"x76"

*Quilters have always used their needles to comment on the times in which they lived. This unknown quiltmaker left a political document marking the presidential election of 1936 in which Kansas Governor Alf Landon unsuccessfully challenged the incumbent Franklin D. Roosevelt. The two candidates' likenesses are embriodered on either side of the U.S. Capitol. This is a two-sided quilt; the back is a pieced 48-star American flag.*

DARTING MINNOWS
Mary McKinstry Hilty
1875-1900
Armstrong County
90"x86"
Catalogue 80.89.3

*The unusual pattern of this intriguing quilt is formed by the sashing; a star design emerges in the piecing of the strips separating the plain squares. By reversing the usual placement of darks and lights, the quiltmaker has turned an ordinary block into a dramatic statement. The navy blue fabric, with its design of comets, is a fine example of the conversational prints popular in the 1880s. The beautiful quilting is highlighted on the back of the quilt where it stands out against the plain muslin fabric.*

DARTING MINNOWS (detail)
Catalogue 80.89.3

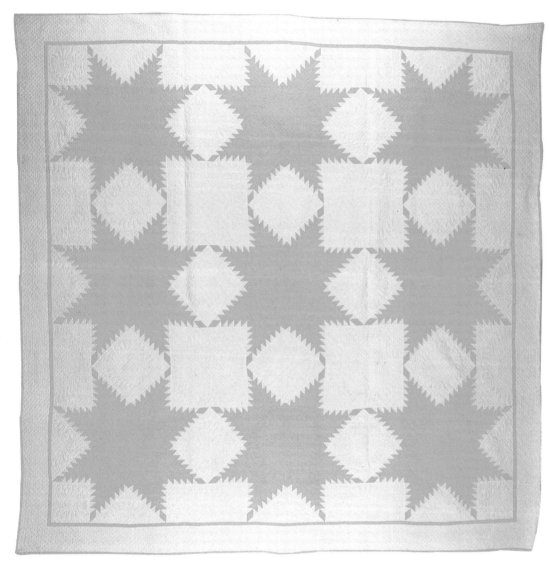

FEATHERED STAR
Rebecca Meredith Jones Fosselman
Circa 1856
Cumberland County
86"x85"
Catalogue 65.62

*This splendidly quilted Feathered Star, one of the most challenging designs to piece, is the work of a master quiltmaker. Feathered wreaths are beautifully quilted in the plain blocks and in the centers of the stars. The choice of yellow for the stars, while logical, was unusual for the period.*

*Catherine Kepner Long,
maker of the Lone Star quilt.*

LONE STAR
Catherine Kepner Long (1832-?)
Circa 1876
Pfouts Valley, Perry County
82"x80"
Catalogue 35.37.17

*This quilt was made for Theodore K. Long, founder of the Carson Long Academy in New Bloomfield, by his mother, Catherine. It is possible that the quilt was cut down from a larger size; the binding appears to date from the 1930s. The background spaces are machine quilted while the star is hand quilted by the piece. The three rows of green diamonds separating the center from the points make the entire star appear to float against the green background.*

ECONOMY PATCH
Maker unknown
1850-1875
84"x78"
Catalogue 42.20.3

*These blocks, also called Square within a Square, were said to have been pieced by ten-year-old David Glenn in 1849. Some of the fabrics do appear to be of that vintage, but others, as well as the green setting blocks, are later. The quilt was probably put together many years after David started the project. Still vibrant, it is a wonderful example of the unpretentious beauty of a scrap quilt.*

*This quilt is made of wool which can be dyed to achieve more saturated colors than cotton. The strong diagonals of color in this Straight Furrow variation of the Log Cabin block add graphic impact to this handsome quilt. It has no batting and minimal quilting and was probably pieced on a foundation block.*

LOG CABIN
Eliza Huber
1850-1900
Lancaster County
80"x69"
Catalogue 76.126

*Emma Ritner, whose father, Joseph, was governor of Pennsylvania from 1835 to 1839, knew that this quilt was her masterpiece. Her name is stamped in four places, lest there be any doubt as to who made it. She used this gorgeous quilt to showcase all her talents. The quilting is exceptional. The piecing of this difficult pattern is precise and she has personalized the design by framing the Sunflowers with gold backgrounds, adding LeMoyne Stars in the sashing and piecing a border of tiny triangles. Emma never married and is buried beside her parents in the Evangelical United Brethren Cemetery in Mountrock, Cumberland County.*

SUNFLOWER
Emma Ritner (1808-1876)
1840-1850
Cumberland County
108"x89"
Catalogue 92.58.1

Silk was being used in American quilts as early as the eighteenth century.[23] The early silk quilts were usually one-patch designs composed of squares, diamonds or hexagons. They seldom combined silk with other fabrics, and were set, bordered, batted, backed and quilted like traditional cotton quilts. Perhaps because of its cost, availability or practicality, silk was never a popular choice for American quilts.

Never, that is, until 1876. It was in that year, at the Centennial Exhibition[24] in Philadelphia, that the American quilting public "discovered" Japan. The Japanese exhibit was extremely popular and inspired Americans to reevaluate their ideas of beauty and design.[25] Irregular shapes and asymmetric designs inspired by the Japanese appeared in wallpapers, fabrics, furniture and furnishings; they also appeared in quiltmaking where they created an entirely new genre, the crazy quilt.

Crazy quilts, sometime called Japanese patchwork or puzzle patchwork in early references,[26] represented a radical departure from traditional quilts in many ways. They used silk, velvet, and other rich fabrics instead of cotton, were composed of irregularly shaped, asymmetrically placed pieces, and employed decorative embroidery. Many had no batting, most had no quilting–they were merely tacked or tied to their protective

backs. In addition, their main purpose was beauty, not warmth. They were made to be decorative throws, carriage robes, table or piano covers, not to cover a bed.

Fueled by the attention of newspaper and magazine writers[27] (who probably were attracted by the name "crazy"), the popularity of crazy quilts made this the dominant style of quiltmaking between 1880 and 1900. Sentimentality contributed to their popularity as well.[28] A crazy quilt enabled the maker to incorporate remembrances of all kinds into her quilt. She could use pieces of clothing; embroider names, initials, or dates; add commemorative ribbons, pictures or purchased embroideries; solicit signatures or sentiments; and compose all of these elements into a beautiful quilt visually held together by the lines of decorative stitching that outlined the pieces.

There were subspecies of crazy quilts, too: ribbon quilts, which used only commemorative ribbons; biscuit quilts, which used large squares of fabric sewn to smaller squares to create little pillows or "biscuits;" and controlled crazy quilts, in which crazy patches were used as pieces in traditional quilt blocks.

After the heyday of crazy quilts, silk was again relegated to a very minor position in the quilt world and practically disappeared during the Depression.

# SILK QUILTS

The collection of silk quilts in The State Museum is both extensive and comprehensive, containing examples that date from the 1830s to the 1920s. The selections that follow are a few of the many beautiful quilts in this category.

CRAZY QUILT (detail)
Catalogue 68.125.6

*Detail of crazy quilt by Annie Rodermel German, pictured on page 47.*

RAIL FENCE
Maker unknown
1838
Probably Bucks County
70"x69"
Catalogue 71.12.3

*This fine Rail Fence is a good example of a pre-crazy silk quilt. Made, according to donor information, in 1838, it contains a wide variety of solids and prints and is backed with yellow silk. There is a heavy batting, probably indicating that, unlike its crazy granddaughters, it was meant to be used for warmth.*

*The crazy quilt on the facing page is set apart from others by the exquisite embroidery covering most of its surface. While almost all crazy quilts have decorative stitching, very few can be compared to this example; the maker was certainly a talented embroiderer who knew how to showcase her ability. In addition to the rows of beautiful stitches, there are embroidered motifs, initials, American flags and fans. Bordered in blue velvet and backed by rose wool, this is a classic, high-style crazy quilt.*

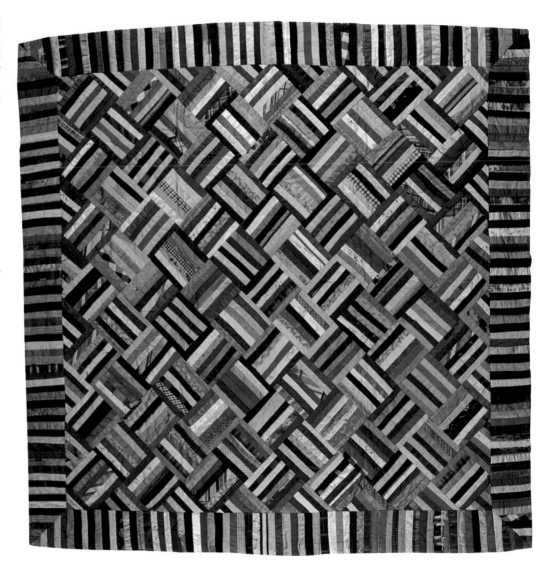

CRAZY QUILT
Maker unknown
1895
Allentown, Lehigh County
64" x 62"
Catalogue 91.101.1

(detail)
Notice the subtle differences between rows of stitches
which, at first glance, seem to be identical.

## CHAPTER 5

DANIEL BOONE LINDERMAN CRAZY QUILT
Amelia Shiery Linderman
1895
Berks County
64"x52"
Catalogue 66.99.146

*This quilt was made for Daniel Boone Linderman by his wife, Amelia Shiery Linderman, in 1895 toward the end of the crazy quilt fad. It was donated to the museum in 1966 by their daughter, Florence A. Linderman. Florence, who was a teacher, missionary (like her parents), and nurse, traveled extensively in America and abroad but still managed to preserve family documents and artifacts until her seventy-third year, when she donated 350 of them to the museum along with a well-annotated inventory. According to her notes, she helped her mother make this quilt. With or without the help of two-year-old Florence, Amelia beautifully embroidered her husband's monogram and the date, and included several patches enhanced with delicate beaded flowers.*

*Amelia Shiery in a photograph taken from her certificate of marriage to Daniel Boone Linderman, January 29, 1891.*

CRAZY QUILT
Annie M. Rodermel German
1884
Harrisburg, Dauphin County
73"x73"
Catalogue 68.125.6

*This is the quintessential crazy quilt. Made by Annie Rodermel German in 1884, it has chenille and dimensional flowers, folded ribbon work, paintings, embroidery, fans, spider webs, and a commemorative ribbon. Unlike other crazy quilts, however, this one was quilted from the back with hand stitching that does not show on the front. The museum also has a silk Rail Fence by Mrs. German (with the same type of quilting) and an 1836 pieced Chimney Sweep by her mother, Harriet Fisher Rodermel.*

CONVENTION RIBBONS QUILT
Ellen Mae Moyer Martz
Circa 1896
Bellwood, Blair County
66"x56"
Catalogue 93.20.1

*Ellen Mae Moyer Martz made this quilt entirely of convention ribbons dating from 1870 to 1896. Although many kinds of ribbons are represented, railroad ribbons predominate. This could be because her husband George was an engineer for the Pennsylvania Railroad. According to family lore, Mrs. Martz had a railroad pass which she used frequently to travel between Altoona and Harrisburg. The pass was returned to the railroad after her coffin was transported from Harrisburg to Bellwood for burial.*

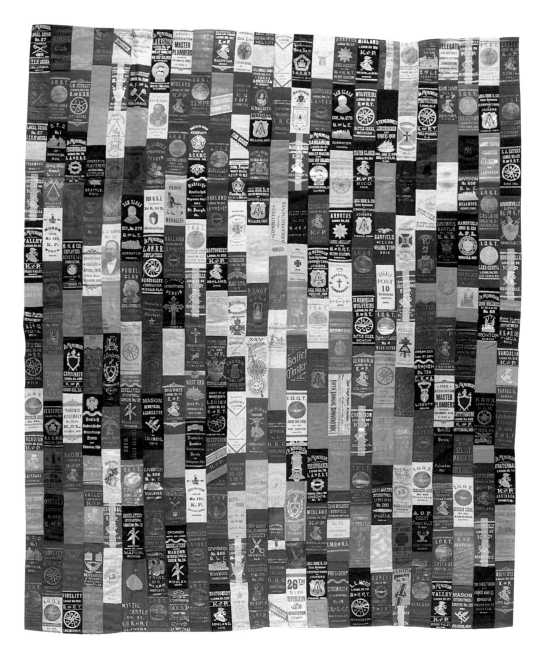

# PARTICULARLY PENNSYLVANIAN

It would be difficult to exaggerate the Pennsylvania influence on the evolution of quiltmaking in America. In this area, as in so many others, Pennsylvania has been the keystone. Before the American Revolution Benjamin Franklin encouraged John Hewson to leave England and settle in Philadelphia where he established a fabric printing business. Hewson produced textiles of the highest quality and elegance, which are found in a number of fine early medallion quilts. *Godey's Lady's Book*, which dictated the taste and fashions of mid-nineteenth-century American women, was published in Philadelphia. The fad for signature quilts which swept the country in the 1840s began among the Quakers of the Delaware Valley.

William Penn's policy of toleration led to immigration by people of different cultures and religions, making Pennsylvania the original American melting pot. These ethnic groups borrowed freely from one another, creating a rich social and artistic environment. While quiltmaking was not a part of the German tradition, Amish, Mennonite, Lutheran and other Pennsylvania German religious groups quickly mastered the craft they had learned from their "English"

neighbors and stamped it with their own aesthetic sensibility, marked by strong colors and innovative designs. Pennsylvania quiltmakers of all ethnic backgrounds used appliqué motifs such as tulips, hearts, birds, and whirligigs which derived from the folk art of the Pennsylvania Germans. As people moved westward in the 1840s and 50s the Pennsylvania influence was felt strongly in Ohio, Indiana, and the Plains States.

The qualities which identify a quilt as particularly Pennsylvanian are many and varied. Color is the most obvious. Certain colors and color combinations are typically Pennsylvanian: double pink and "poison" green, the rich colors of the Amish quilts, the pink, orange, green, and red of the floral appliqués, the distinctive bright blue which appears frequently in quilts made in Berks and surrounding counties, and bold pumpkin yellow used as a background color.

The defining characteristic can be the way the quilt is constructed. Quilts made of four large blocks, often elaborate floral designs with extravagant borders, but sometimes a free-form

eagle, are typically Pennsylvanian.[29] Zigzag sashing and borders are a common design choice. Strippy quilts set with the blocks in vertical rows, and quilts with backs pieced in strips of different fabrics were most often made in southeastern Pennsylvania. Pieced pillowcases were made almost exclusively by the Pennsylvania Germans as an extension of their custom of decorating pillowcases with embroidery.[30]

Some quilts identify themselves at first glance as part of the Pennsylvania tradition. The collection of The State Museum contains some wonderful examples.

STAR OF BETHLEHEM MEDALLION
Matilda Ripple Nevin (1811- ?)
1840-1850
Franklin County
92"x91"
Catalogue 80.42

*It is difficult to imagine a more lavish star quilt than this mid-nineteenth-century masterpiece executed by Matilda Ripple Nevin. A large star is used as a central medallion surrounded by a border of diamonds an' twenty-six smaller stars in three different sizes. The final touch of elegance is a wide chintz border enhanced by half-square triangles. This quilt combines the medallion and the repeat-block styles. Matilda used the Pennsylvania German palette to achieve a pulsating effect in the large central star. The quilt contains a fascinating collection of early fabrics in pristine condition. (See detail on page 33.)*

*Rebecca Kohler made the delightful original design quilt on the facing page for her son Jacob who was born in 1832. Radiating from a central star are pieced and appliquéd blocks of varying sizes. The tulip and whirligig motifs are typically Pennsylvania German. The back of the quilt is an imported green pillar print (see detail), a very expensive fabric popular in the 1820s and 30s. This is a summer spread made without batting or quilting.*[31]

ORIGINAL DESIGN BABY QUILT
Rebecca Kohler
Circa 1832
Berks County
43"x41"
Catalogue 29.35

(detail of back)
Catalogue 29.35

FLYING EAGLE
Catherine Gudila Burgaman Swengel (1832-1872)
Circa 1870
83"X81"
Catalogue 65.38.2

*The eagle has been a favorite American decorative motif since the days of the Revolution. Eagle quilts were particularly popular in Pennsylvania, where many examples extraordinarily similar to one another have been found. The general appearance of the eagle, with its shield-shaped body, is almost identical in these quilts, although details such as the position of the feet or objects held in the beak or talons may differ. The pattern was probably taken from the eagle on the Great Seal of the United States pictured below.*

*This typical Pennsylvania eagle quilt has four large blocks oriented toward the central star which gives a playful look to the stylized eagles. A baby quilt made by Catherine Swengel is pictured on page 35.*

EAGLES AND ROSES
Mother of Agnes Delilah Dice
Circa 1859
94"x94"
Catalogue 64.64.7

*This quilt in which a row of eagle blocks alternates with a row of diagonally crossed roses is a striking combination of two traditional designs. It is further embellished with small appliqued circles. The overall sensibility of this quilt is more formal than that of the typical four-block eagle quilt. It was made to celebrate the birth of Agnes Delilah Dice whose name and birthday, Sept. 3, 1859, were embroidered on the top after it was quilted.*

PRINCE GALLITZIN'S QUILT
Maker Unknown
Circa 1840
Loretto, Cambria County
72"x62"
Catalogue 70.29.8

*This Prince's Feather[32] quilt must once have been a fine example of the Pennsylvania four-block style. Even in its badly worn and faded condition, with its borders missing, it is of great interest because of its association with an important figure in Pennsylvania history. Demetrius Gallitzin was a Russian prince who became a Catholic priest and served as a missionary in the wilds of Pennsylvania. In 1799 he founded the town of Loretto in the mountains west of Altoona and lived there until his death in 1840. This quilt, which descended in a family who were among the earliest settlers in Loretto, is said to have been designed by the Prince and made under his direction. The name Prince's Feather has nothing to do with Prince Gallitzin; it probably refers to the feathers in the crest of the Prince of Wales.[33] The appliqué motifs are made of an overdyed green (blue fabric dyed yellow to make green) which indicates an early date.*

FLYING GEESE
Mary Kieffer
1875-1900
92"x74"
Catalogue 31.64

*This is a fine example of a strippy quilt with the "geese" set in vertical bars of the strong colors typical of eastern Pennsylvania. An indication of the date is provided by the quilt back (see detail), which is printed with cannon and flags; the Centennial of 1876 inspired many fabrics in patriotic designs.*

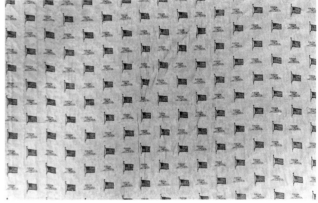

(detail of back)
Catalogue 31.64

BARS (detail)
Maker unknown
Circa 1920
Lancaster County
76"x68"
Catalogue 76.222.1

SUNSHINE AND SHADOW
Mary Zook
1926
Lancaster County
77"x76"
Catalogue 76.222.3

DIAMOND IN A SQUARE
Maker Unknown
Circa 1920
Lancaster County
75"x74"
Catalogue 76.222.2

*To many people, Pennsylvania quilts mean Amish quilts, although Amish quilts made before the late nineteenth century are rare. The Amish style is unmistakable, distinguished by simple piecing, strong colors, and elaborate quilting. The Sunshine and Shadow, Diamond in the Square, and Bars patterns are associated almost exclusively with the Amish of Lancaster County. Only solid-color fabrics were used on the front of quilts, in a palette ranging from red through purple to dark green, the colors found in the clothing of the Amish people. Dark thread was most often used for the quilting and bindings were usually wide and unstuffed. These traditional Amish quilts are stunning in their bold simplicity.*

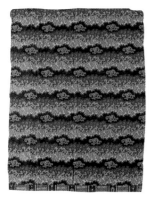 

OHIO STAR PIECED PILLOWCASES (front, back)
Maker unknown
1825-1840
18"x24"
Catalogue 24.11.16

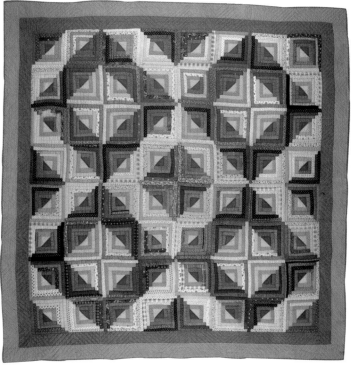

LOG CABIN
Maker unknown
1890-1920
81"x 80"
Catalogue 73.98.488

*Pieced pillowcases are rare and have been made almost exclusively by Pennsylvania German women who brought from Europe a tradition of embellishing pillowcases with embroidery. As they learned quilting from their "English" neighbors they began to decorate pillowcases with patchwork and appliqué, sometimes to complement a quilt in the same design. These pillowcases were probably only for decoration and would have been removed at night.[34]*

*The Log Cabin pattern embodies the popular conception of the American quilt. Made of scraps of fabric to serve a practical purpose, the blocks can be combined in many different sets. This Barn Raising variation is a true scrap quilt, which contains an interesting collection of late nineteenth-century conversational prints and shirting fabrics as well as calicoes. It is obvious that the maker carefully planned her project. The center or chimney of each block is unusual because it is made of blue and yellow triangles rather than the traditional red square. The back of the quilt is pieced in broad strips of double pink and a striking shade of bright blue (sometimes called oil-boiled blue). Both the pieced back and the colors are typical of quilts made in southeastern Pennsylvania.*

STAR OF BETHLEHEM
Sally Albright
Circa 1900
West Hanover Township, Dauphin County
87"x86"
Catalogue 31.96.17

*The Pennsylvania German influence on this quilt is unmistakable. The choice of pumpkin yellow for the background is particularly effective. The top was pieced by Sally Albright and quilted by a Mrs. Moyer, who because of her expert quilting was known as "Quilt Moyer." Her talent is evident in the elaborate designs executed in a fine, regular quilting stitch. Sally Albright was justifiably proud of her dramatic star quilt; it came to The State Museum with a tag attached to the back which reads, "Save for the People of Pennsylvania."*

**Album quilt**. Quilt composed of blocks of different designs (sometimes signed) often made by more than one person.

**Appliqué**. Designs cut from one fabric and stitched to another.

**Batting**. The filler, usually cotton, wool or more recently polyester, which is the center of the quilt "sandwich," i.e., the layer between the top and back.

**Broderie Perse**. A technique in which printed motifs are cut from fabric, usually chintz, and then appliqued to a background fabric.

**Chintz**. High-quality, imported cotton fabric, often with a floral pattern, which was usually glazed.

**Conversational prints**. Small-scale print fabrics, usually in two colors, of recognizable objects such as cannon, comets, horseshoes and arrows, etc. They were popular in the 1880s.

**Copperplate**. A method which used incised plates to print fabric with a fine-line design, almost always in a single color.

**Double pink**. Popular bright pink tone-on-tone prints in small-scale designs, produced continuously since the middle of the nineteenth century.

**English paper piecing**. Technique in which fabric is basted over paper templates; the shapes are then whip-stitched together. It is often used to piece small shapes with precision.

(detail)
Catalogue 81.10

**Friendship quilt**. Quilt made of signed blocks, intended as remembrances. The blocks can either be pieced or appliqued and are usually of the same pattern.

**Medallion**. Quilt design in which a central motif is surrounded by multiple borders.

**Overdyed**. Process in which fabric is dyed twice to achieve a third color. For example, fabric is dyed blue and then yellow, or vice versa, to achieve green.

**Pieced/patchwork**. Pieces cut from different fabrics and sewn together to form designs, usually geometric.

**Pillar prints**. Imported fabric printed with large architectural columns and usually decorated with floral designs, popular between 1810 and 1835.

**Quilt**. A three-layer fabric sandwich composed of a top, batting and a back, usually held together by ties or stitching.

**Quilting**. A regular, small, running stitch used to hold the quilt top, batting and back together.

**Quilting by the piece**. Quilting around the individual shapes which make up a quilt block.

**Roller print**. Fabric printing technique using engraved copper cylinders. The technology revolutionized textile production by making fabric printing faster and more efficient.

**Sampler**. A quilt composed of blocks of different designs.

**Sash**. Strips of fabric which separate blocks in a quilt top.

**Set**. The way in which quilt blocks are put together.

**Stippled**. Very close quilting done in a meandering design.

**Strippy**. A quilt top or back which is pieced in wide strips of different fabrics. This also refers to blocks which are set in this manner.

**Stuffed**. A quilting design which is padded with extra batting so that it is raised. It is sometimes referred to as *trapunto*.

**Summer spread**. A quilt top which is backed but has neither batting nor quilting.

**Turkey red**. The color produced by an expensive dye process that resulted in a fabric which did not bleed or fade. It was widely available by the 1840s.

**Utility quilting**. Quilting done primarily to hold the quilt sandwich together, characterized by widely spaced, simple designs.

**Pieced Pillowcases**
1825-1850
Maker unknown
Cotton
Catalogue 24.11.1

**Bureau Scarf**
Circa 1810
Mary Elmaker Kapp
Harrisburg, Dauphin Co.
Cotton
Catalogue 28.12.66

**Bureau Scarf**
Circa 1810
Mary Elmaker Kapp
Harrisburg, Dauphin Co.
Cotton
Catalogue 28.12.67

**Bureau Scarf**
Circa 1810
Mary Elmaker Kapp
Harrisburg, Dauphin Co.
Cotton
Catalogue 28.12.68

**Amos Kapp's Cradle Quilt**
1809
Kitty Dupes
Harrisburg, Dauphin Co.
Cotton
Catalogue 29.30.5

**Original Design Baby Quilt**
Circa 1832
Rebecca Kohler
Berks Co.
Cotton
Catalogue 29.35

**Hexagon Quilt**
1814
Catharine Kapp
Harrisburg, Dauphin Co.
Cotton
Catalogue 31.63.6

**Flying Geese**
1875-1900
Mary Kieffer
Cotton
Catalogue 31.64

**LeMoyne Star Quilt Top**
1825-1850
Maker unknown
Cotton
Catalogue 31.69.11

**Carolina Lily**
1850-1875
Maker unknown
New Freedom, York Co.
Cotton
Catalogue 31.96.14

**Lemoyne Star Friendship Quilt**
Circa 1850
Maker unknown
Cotton
Catalogue 31.96.15

**Honey Bee**
1850-1875
Maker unknown
Cotton
Catalogue 31.96.16

**Star of Bethlehem**
Circa 1900
Sally Albright
West Hanover Township, Dauphin Co.
Cotton
Catalogue 31.96.17

**Star of Bethlehem**
Circa 1900
Sally Albright
West Hanover Township, Dauphin Co.
Cotton
Catalogue 31.96.18

**Basket**
1875-1925
Maker unknown
Cotton
Catalogue 31.96.19

**Log Cabin**
1850-1900
Maker unknown
Silk
Catalogue 33.36.67

**LeMoyne Star**
1880-1900
Maker unknown
Cotton
Catalogue 33.36.68

**Lily Friendship Quilt Top**
Circa 1879
Elizabeth Reininger Shriver
Bedford or Fulton Co.
Cotton
Catalogue 34.38

**Crazy**
1880-1900
Maker unknown
Silk, wool, velvet
Catalogue 34.129.34

**Lone Star**
Circa 1876
Maker: Catherine Kepner Long
Pfouts Valley, Perry Co.
Cotton
Catalogue 35.37.17

**Star of Bethlehem**
Circa 1850
Maker unknown
Cotton
Catalogue 36.1.1

**Chimney Sweep**
1825-1850
Maker unknown
Cotton
Catalogue 36.11

**Fleur de Lis**
Circa 1850
Daughter of John McCreight
Cotton
Catalogue 37.2.1

**Medallion Baby Quilt**
1825-1850
Maker unknown
Cotton
Catalogue 40.24.83

**Medallion Baby Quilt**
1850-1900
Maker unknown
Cotton
Catalogue 40.24.84

**Whitework with Sashing**
Circa 1850
Maker unknown
Cotton
Catalogue 40.43.2

**Economy Patch**
1850-1875
Maker unknown
Cotton
Catalogue 42.20.3

**Carolina Lily**
Circa 1850
Maker unknown
Cotton
Catalogue 42.20.4

**Box in a Box Doll Quilt**
1875-1900
Maker unknown
Cotton
Catalogue 43.2.8

**Chintz Doll Quilt**
Circa 1850
Maker unknown
Cotton
Catalogue 43.2.116B

**Chintz Medallion**
1825-1850
Alice Cochran
Cotton
Catalogue 44.27

**Log Cabin**
1900-1920
Barbara Clara Beard
Wool, velvet, rayon, linen
Catalogue 46.19

**President's Wreath**
Circa 1850
Maker unknown
Cotton
Catalogue 46.22.1

**Log Cabin**
Circa 1900
Maker unknown
Silk, velvet
Catalogue 47.2

**Prince's Feather**
Circa 1870
Alinda Jane Potts
Cotton
Catalogue 49.21.71

**Embroidered Quilt**
Circa 1930
Alinda Jane Potts
Cotton
Catalogue 49.21.72

**One Patch**
1900-1925
Maker unknown
Cotton
Catalogue 50.45.46

**Birds in Flight**
1875-1900
Nancy Stoops
Cotton
Catalogue 57.3.5

**LeMoyne Star**
1875-1900
Nancy Stoops
Cotton
Catalogue 57.3.6

**Blazing Star**
Circa 1920
Nancy Patterson
New Castle, Lawrence Co.
Cotton, wool, rayon
Catalogue 58.8

**Carolina Lily**
Circa 1850
Maker unknown
Cotton
Catalogue 60.55.1

**Cactus**
Circa 1860
Elizabeth Smith
Newport, Perry Co.
Cotton
Catalogue 61.54.6

**Delectable Mountains**
1846
F. Cayette Lesher
Cotton
Catalogue 62.25

**Carolina Lily**
Circa 1880
Maker unknown
Cotton
Catalogue 63.46.1

**Jacob's Ladder**
1875-1900
G.A. Burgh
Pottsville, Schuylkill Co.
Cotton
Catalogue 63.46.2

Rose of Sharon
Circa 1853
Eliza Cooper
Cotton
Catalogue 63.49

Orange Peel
1900-1925
Maker unknown
Cotton
Catalogue 63.56.1

Pieced Pillowcases
1850-1875
Maker unknown
Cotton
Catalogue 63.56.3
Catalogue 63.56.4

Pieced Bag
Circa 1860
Maker unknown
Cotton
Catalogue 63.56.6

Caesar's Crown
Circa 1850
Maker unknown
Cotton
Catalogue 64.39.3

Lily
1875-1900
Maker unknown
Cotton
Catalogue 64.55.1

Baskets
Circa 1930
Maker unknown
Cotton
Catalogue 64.55.2

Irish Chain
Circa 1900
Maker unknown
Cotton
Catalogue 64.56.48

Crazy
1880-1900
Maker unknown
Silk, velvet
Catalogue 64.56.49

Eagles and Roses
Circa 1859
Mother of Agnes Delilah
    Dice
Cotton
Catalogue 64.64.7

Log Cabin Quilt Top
1850-1900
Maker unknown
Silk
Catalogue 64.73.1

Crazy
Circa 1900
Maker unknown
Silk, rayon, velvet, wool
Catalogue 65.36.1

Birds in Flight Baby Quilt
1850-1900
Catherine Gudila Bergaman
    Swengel
Cotton
Catalogue 65.38.1

Flying Eagle
Circa 1870
Catherine Gudila Bergaman
    Swengel
Cotton
Catalogue 65.38.2

Feathered Star
Circa 1856
Rebecca Meridith Jones
    Fosselman
Cumberland Co.
Cotton
Catalogue 65.62

Wickersham Album Quilt
Circa 1854
Rebecca Garretson
    Wickersham
Newberry Township, York Co.
Cotton
Catalogue 65.78

Variable Star
Circa 1860
Maker unknown
Schuylkill Co.
Cotton
Catalogue 65.119

Crazy
1880-1900
Maker unknown
Silk, velvet
Catalogue 66.16.2

Biscuit
1890-1910
Maker unknown
Silk
Catalogue 66.41.19

Doll's Mattress and Quilt
Circa 1900
Amelia Shiery Linderman
Berks Co.
Cotton
Catalogue 66.99.23

Crazy
1895
Amelia Shiery Linderman
Berks Co.
Silk, velvet
Catalogue 66.99.146

Crazy
1880-1900
Maker unknown
Velvet
Catalogue 67.108.10

Crazy
1888-1910
Deborah M. Gibson
Lancaster, Lancaster Co.
Silk, velvet
Catalogue 68.70

Rolling Stone Signature
    Quilt
1852
Caroline Brobst
Lynn Township, Lehigh Co.
Cotton
Catalogue 68.78

Chimney Sweep
1825-1850
Harriet Fisher Rodermel
Cotton
Catalogue 68.125.1

Crazy
Circa 1884
Annie Rodermel German
Harrisburg, Dauphin Co.
Silk, velvet
Catalogue 68.125.6

Rail Fence
1880-1900
Annie Rodermel German
Harrisburg, Dauphin Co.
Silk, velvet
Catalogue 68.125.7

Orange Peel
Circa 1900
Sisters of John Eby
Zion, Centre County
Cotton
Catalogue 68.132.1

Crazy
1880-1900
Maker unknown
Silk, velvet
Catalogue 68.133.1

Orange Peel
1825-1850
Maker unknown
Cotton
Catalogue 69.19.7

Crazy
1880-1900
Maker unknown
Silk, velvet
Catalogue 69.19.8

Log Cabin
1900-1925
Maker unknown
Silk
Catalogue 69.42

Whitework
1820-1850
S.W. Adams
Cotton
Catalogue 69.116

Delectable Mountains
Circa 1900
Maker unknown
Cotton
Catalogue 70.12.1

Prince's Feather
Circa 1840
Maker unknown
Loretto, Cambria Co.
Cotton
Catalogue 70.29.8

Medallion
Circa 1800
Virginia Robinson Drum
Pittsburgh, Allegheny Co.
Cotton
Catalogue 70.50.8

Tulips and Berries
Circa 1850
Maker unknown
Cotton
Catalogue 70.50.9

Crazy
1890-1920
Mother of Ruth Ruef
Silk, velvet
Catalogue 70.50.10

Crazy
1890-1900
Charlotte Elizabeth Coblentz
Middleton, Maryland
Silk, satin, velvet
Catalogue 70.50.11

Log Cabin
1890-1920
Maker unknown
Cotton, rayon, wool
Catalogue 70.99

Baskets
Circa 1930
Maker unknown
Cotton
Catalogue 70.104.7

Baskets
Circa 1900
Maker unknown
Cotton
Catalogue 70.104.8

Rail Fence
Circa 1840
Maker unknown
Probably Bucks Co.
Silk
Catalogue 71.12.3

Roses
Circa 1850
Barbara Smith Scholl
Cotton
Catalogue 71.12.4

**Basket Baby Quilt**
Circa 1850
Sarah Schutt
Bucks County
Cotton
Catalogue 71.12.5

**Crazy, unfinished**
1887
Maker unknown
Juniata Co.
Silk, velvet
Catalogue 71.12.37

**Masonic Ribbons**
Circa 1890
Probably Anna A. Garner
  Scholl
Cotton, silk
Catalogue 71.12.38

**Nine Patch**
1875-1900
Maker unknown
Cotton
Catalogue 71.34.1

**Chimney Sweep**
1850-1875
Maker unknown
Cotton
Catalogue 71.34.2

**Zig Zag**
1850-1900
Maker unknown
Cotton
Catalogue 71.34.3

**Carpenter's Wheel**
Circa 1930
Maker unknown
Cotton
Catalogue 71.34.4

**Crazy**
1889
Maker unknown
Silk, velvet
Catalogue 71.34.7

**Log Cabin**
1900-1920
Maker unknown
Cotton, rayon, wool, silk
Catalogue 71.34.8

**Log Cabin**
Circa 1900
Maker unknown
Wool, cotton
Catalogue 71.34.9

**Cherry Wreath**
Circa 1850
Maker unknown
Cotton
Catalogue 71.49.1

**Sunburst**
1850-1875
Maker unknown
Cotton
Catalogue 71.59

**Sunburst**
1850-1875
Maker unknown
Cotton
Catalogue 71.71.11

**Black-Eyed Susan**
Circa 1860
Margaret Cooper Cooper
Butler Co.
Cotton
Catalogue 71.89

**President's Wreath Baby
  Quilt**
1850-1875
Maker unknown
Cotton
Catalogue 72.11.1

**Variable Star**
1875-1900
Landis-Piper Family
Newville, Cumberland Co.
Cotton
Catalogue 72.190.1

**Nine Patch**
Circa 1900
Landis-Piper Family
Newville, Cumberland Co.
Cotton
Catalogue 72.190.2

**Ocean Waves Baby Quilt**
Circa 1900
Maker unknown
Cotton
Catalogue 73.60.24

**Feathered Star**
1800-1825
Maker unknown
Cotton
Catalogue 73.98.181

**Biscuit**
Circa 1900
Maker unknown
Velvet
Catalogue 73.98.241

**Log Cabin**
1890-1900
Maker unknown
Cotton
Catalogue 73.98.488

**Tulips**
1850-1900
Maker unknown
Cotton
Catalogue 73.146.5

**Crazy**
1880-1900
Maker unknown
Silk, velvet, satin
Catalogue 73.203

**Endless Chain**
Circa 1930
Maker unknown
Cotton
Catalogue 73.220

**Crazy**
1888
Maker unknown
Silk, velvet
Catalogue 74.2

**Bricks**
1900-1925
Maker unknown
Wool
Catalogue 74.49.87

**Irish Chain**
Circa 1920
Maker unknown
Cotton
Catalogue 74.49.89

**Baskets**
Circa 1930
Maker unknown
Cotton
Catalogue 74.84

**Basket Signature Quilt**
1875-1900
Maker unknown
Perry County
Cotton
Catalogue 74.163.1

**Baby Blocks**
1880-1900
Maker unknown
Silk
Catalogue 74.163.2

**Penny Squares**
Circa 1883
Laura Hood
Cotton
Catalogue 74.166.1

**Eagle**
1962
Mabel Hess
Camp Hill, Cumberland Co.
Cotton
Catalogue 75.2

**Bicentennial Quilt**
1975
Brownie Troop 42
Conewago Township,
York Co.
Cotton, polyester
Catalogue 75.43

**Drunkard's Path**
Circa 1920
Mrs. Jacob O. Reed
Cotton
Catalogue 75.45

**Triple Irish Chain**
1850-1875
Maker unknown
Cotton
Catalogue 75.74

**Peony Friendship Quilt**
1847
Salem German Reformed
  Church
Harrisburg, Dauphin Co.
Cotton
Catalogue 76.65

**Pennsylvania Star**
1975
Gloria Bubeck
Kunkletown, Monroe Co.
Cotton, polyester
Catalogue 76.91

**Bicentennial Quilt**
1976
Benjamin Franklin Elemen-
tary School
Harrisburg, Dauphin Co.
Cotton, polyester
Catalogue 76.92

**Laurel Leaf**
1847
Sabina Oberly
Northampton Co.
Cotton
Catalogue 76.94

**Log Cabin**
1850-1900
Eliza Huber
Lancaster, Lancaster Co.
Wool
Catalogue 76.126

**Hexagon Top**
Circa 1868
Maker unknown
Cotton
Catalogue 76.137

**Laurel Leaf**
Circa 1850
Maker unknown
Cotton
Catalogue 76.169.1

**Variable Star**
Circa 1880
Maker unknown
Cotton
Catalogue 76.169.2

**Baby Blocks**
Circa 1860
Maker unknown
Silk
Catalogue 76.209

**Bars**
Circa 1920
Maker unknown
Lancaster Co.
Wool
Catalogue 76.222.1

Diamond in the Square
Circa 1920
Maker unknown
Lancaster Co.
Wool
Catalogue 76.222.2

Sunshine and Shadow
1926
Mary Zook
Lancaster Co.
Cotton, wool
Catalogue 76.222.3

Bicentennial Quilt
1976
Pine Street Presbyterian
   Church
Harrisburg, Dauphin Co.
Cotton, polyester
Catalogue 76.239

Embroidered Eagle
1976
Pennsylvania State
   Society, Daughters of
   the American Revolution
Cotton
Catalogue 77.9

Bicentennial Quilt
1976
Washington School
Sand Point, Idaho
Cotton, polyester
Catalogue 77.31.18

Whitework
Circa 1820
Isabella McConnell Criswell
Cotton
Catalogue 77.190.92

Roosevelt-Landon Quilt
Circa 1936
Maker unknown
Bradford Co.
Cotton
Catalogue 78.101.4

Crown of Thorns
Circa 1881
Linda Bell Statler Picking
Chambersburg, Franklin Co.
Cotton
Catalogue 78.136

Broderie Perse Summer
   Spread
Circa 1828
Jane Griffith Roberts
Harrisburg, Dauphin Co.
Cotton
Catalogue 79.99.1

Star of Bethlehem Medallion
1840-1850
Matilda Ripple Nevin
Franklin County
Cotton
Catalogue 80.42

One Patch
1900-1925
Maker unknown
Cotton, rayon
Catalogue 80.54.1

Log Cabin Top
1890-1900
Florence Devinney
Lebanon, Lebanon Co.
Wool
Catalogue 80.67

Churn Dash
1875-1900
Wool
Catalogue 80.89.2

Darting Minnows
Circa 1880
Mary McKinstry Hilty
Armstrong Co.
Cotton
Catalogue 80.89.3

Whitework
Circa 1820
Hannah Welsh Dingee
York, York Co.
Cotton
Catalogue 81.10

Churn Dash
1875-1900
Carlisle, Cumberland Co.
Cotton
Catalogue 83.42.1

Whitework
Circa 1826
Maker unknown
Cotton
Catalogue 83.42.2

Crazy
Circa 1900
Maria Mead Smith
Silk, velvet
Catalogue 83.42.3

Feathered Star
1825-1850
Maker unknown
Cotton
Catalogue 83.58

Mariner's Compass Friend-
   ship Quilt
Circa 1850
Euphemia Wilson Righter
Beaver Meadow, Carbon Co.
Cotton
Catalogue 83.69

Box in a Box Baby Quilt
1900-1925
Mrs. Christian Laubach
Northampton Co.
Cotton
Catalogue 84.67

Album Quilt
Circa 1854
Shunk Family
Upper Providence Township,
   Montgomery Co.
Cotton
Catalogue BB85.1.32

Crazy, unfinished
1880-1900
Maker unknown
Cotton, silk
Catalogue 85.130

Crazy
1875-1900
Anna Markle Kain
Philadelphia
Cotton, wool, silk, velvet
Catalogue 86.72

Four Patch Baby Quilt
1870-1880
Maker unknown
Cotton, wool
Catalogue 87.30.9

Chintz Medallion Baby
   Quilt
1825-1850
Maker unknown
Cotton
Catalogue 87.75

Crazy
1899
Maud Susan Groninger
Port Royal, Juniata Co.
Silk, velvet
Catalogue 89.8

Masonic Ribbons
Circa 1900
Laura Julia Clauss Ash
Lehighton, Carbon Co.
Silk
Catalogue 90.2.9

Crazy
Circa 1895
Maker unknown
Allentown, Lehigh Co.
Silk, velvet
Catalogue 91.101.1

Sunflower
1825-1850
Emma Ritner
Mountrock, Cumberland Co.
Cotton
Catalogue 92.58.1

Convention Ribbons
Circa 1896
Ellen Mae Moyer Martz
Bellwood, Blair Co.
Silk
Catalogue 93.20.1

Jacob's Ladder
Circa 1850
Maker unknown
Cotton
Catalogue JT76.10

Chain
1850-1875
Maker unknown
Cotton
Catalogue JT77.2

Wholecloth
1780-1800
Maker unknown
Wool
Catalogue PG75.35

Whig Rose
Circa 1850
Maker unknown
Cotton
Catalogue SH65.1

Crazy
Circa 1900
Maker unknown
Cotton, wool, silk, velvet
Catalogue SH65.97

Baby Block
1850-1875
Maker unknown
Cotton
Catalogue SH69.324

Peony
Circa 1855
Mary Ann Beighley
Cotton
Catalogue SH70.341

Star Variation
1850-1900
Maker unknown
Cotton
Catalogue SH70.352

Postage Stamp
1900-1925
Maker unknown
Cotton, rayon
Catalogue SH76.16

Flying Geese Baby Quilt
Circa 1890
Maker unknown
Cotton
Catalogue SH76.29

Twenty-five Patch Baby
   Quilt
Circa 1880
Maker unknown
Cotton
Catalogue SH76.272

**Nine Patch**
Circa 1850
Maker unknown
Cotton
Catalogue VF72.135

**Toile de Jouy**
1825-1850
Maker unknown
Cotton
Catalogue VF74.51

**Irish Chain**
1850-1900
Maker unknown
Cotton
Catalogue VF74.52

**Sunburst**
1875-1900
Maker unknown
Cotton
Catalogue VF74.53

**Variable Star**
1850-1900
Maker unknown
Cotton
Catalogue VF74.54

**Whig Rose**
1850-1875
Maker unknown
Cotton
Catalogue VF74.55

**LeMoyne Star**
1900-1950
Maker unknown
Cotton
Catalogue VF74.56

**Bars**
1880-1900
Maker unknown
Wool
Not Catalogued

**Log Cabin**
1850-1900
Maker unknown
Silk
Not Catalogued

**Crazy**
Circa 1900
Maker unknown
Silk, velvet, rayon
Not Catalogued

**Carpenter's Wheel**
Circa 1850
Maker unknown
Cotton
Not Catalogued

**One Patch**
1900-1940
Maker unknown
Cotton
Not Catalogued

**Crazy**
1880-1900
Maker unknown
Cotton, silk, velvet
Not Catalogued

**Broken Dishes**
1880-1900
Maker unknown
Silk
Not Catalogued

**Bricks**
Circa 1900
Maker unknown
Wool
Not Catalogued

(detail)
Catalogue 81.10

**Blocks**
Circa 1900
Maker unknown
Silk
Not Catalogued

**Log Cabin**
Circa 1900
Maker unknown
Silk, velvet
Not Catalogued

**Whitework**
1825-1875
Maker unknown
Cotton
Catalogue X85.3

**Fleur de Lis**
Circa 1860
Maker unknown
Cotton
Catalogue X86.28.9

**Whitework**
1825-1875
Maker unknown
Cotton
Catalogue X86.33.1

**Four Patch**
1880-1900
Maker unknown
Cotton
Catalogue X86.33.2

**Lone Star**
1900-1930
Maker unknown
Cotton
Catalogue X86.33.3

**Triangles**
Circa 1900
Maker unknown
Cotton
Catalogue X86.33.4

If you would like more information about quilts in this collection, please contact The State Museum of Pennsylvania at P.O. Box 1026, Harrisburg, PA 17108-1026, or telephone (717) 787-4980, TDD (800) 654-5984.

1. Barbara Brackman, *Clues in the Calico* (McLean, Va.: EPM Publications, Inc., 1989), 112.

2. Roderick Kiracofe, *The American Quilt: A History of Cloth and Comfort, 1750-1950* (New York: Clarkson Potter Publishers, 1993), 48.

3. Ibid., 61.

4. Patricia T. Herr, *"The Ornamental Branches": Needlework and Arts from the Lititz Moravian Girls' School, between 1800 and 1865* (Virginia Beach: The Donning Company, 1996), 13.

5. Ibid., 18.

6. Kiracofe, *The American Quilt*, 81.

7. *History of Beaver Meadows, Carbon County.* In commemoration of its Sesquicentennial, 11.

8. Robert L. Robinson, *The Wickersham Letters, 1849-1887* (1984), 55.

9. Conversation with Patricia T. Herr, March 6, 1996.

10. Jeana Kimball, *Red and Green: An Applique Tradition*, (Bothell, Wash.: That Patchwork Place, Inc., 1990), 8.

11. Linda Giesler Carlson, *Roots, Feathers and Blooms: 4-Block Quilts, Their History & Patterns, Book I*, (Paducah, Ky.: American Quilter's Society, 1994), 112.

12. Barbara Brackman, et al., *Kansas Quilts and Quilters*, (Lawrence: University Press of Kansas , 1993), 89.

13. Ricky Clark, ed., *Quilts in Community: Ohio's Traditions*, (Nashville: Rutledge Hill Press, 1991), 24.

14. Brackman, et al., *Kansas Quilts and Quilters*, 89. In the Kansas study, there were numerous examples of the routes taken by makers of red-and-green quilts. In three examples cited in the book, the families had first settled in Pennsylvania, traveled to Ohio, and then gone on to Kansas. The families were from Northumberland, Lancaster and York Counties.

15. Ibid.

16. Barbara Brackman, *Encyclopedia of Appliqué* (McLean,Va.: EPM Publications, Inc., 1993), 80. This design is #19.42.

17. *Historical Review of Berks County*, 58, 1 (Winter 1992-1993), 16.

18. Jeannette Lasansky, *Pieced By Mother: Over 100 Years of Quiltmaking Traditions*, (Lewisburg, Pa.: Oral Traditions Project of the Union County Historical Society, 1988), 53. Although this quilt is a four-block quilt and uses the Cactus pattern, it has only one complete "Cactus" in the center, so it takes on a completely different look.

19. Mary Elizabeth Johnson, *Star Quilts*, (New York: Clarkson Potter Publishers, 1992), 11.

20. Patsy and Myron Orlofsky, *Quilts in America* (New York: McGraw-Hill Book Company, 1974), 49.

21. Wilene Smith, "Quilt Blocks or Quilt Patterns," in *Quiltmaking in America: Beyond the Myths* (Nashville: Rutledge Hill Press, 1994), 34.

22. Barbara Brackman, *Encyclopedia of Pieced Quilt Patterns* (Paducah, Ky.: American Quilter's Society, 1993), 55. A similar quilt is illustrated on page 134 of *Florida Quilts*. The Florida quilt is called Wagon Wheel.

23. Orlofsky, *Quilts in America*, 208.

24. Although "Exhibition" and "Exposition" have been used interchangeably for the 1876 event, its official name was the Centennial Exhibition. See *The Centennial Exhibition* and *Illustrated Guide to Fairmount Park and the Centennial Exhibition*, both published in 1876.

25. Penny McMorris, *Crazy Quilts* (New York: E.P. Dutton, Inc., 1984), 12.

26. Ibid., 11.

27. Brackman, *Clues in the Calico*, 25.

28. Kiracofe, *The American Quilt*, 146.

29. Carlson, *Roots, Feathers and Blooms*, 112.

30. Tandy Hirsh, "The Evolution of the Pennsylvania-German Pillowcase," in *Bits and Pieces: Textile Traditions* (Lewisburg, Pa.: Oral Traditions Project of the Union County Historical Society, 1991), 44.

31. This quilt is pictured on page 89 of Orlofsky, *Quilts in America*.

32. Ricky Clark, *Quilted Gardens* (Nashville: Rutledge Hill Press, 1994), 37-41. This design is sometimes called Princess Feather, a name which is also applied to the undulating feather design often quilted in borders.

33. Carlson, *Roots, Feathers and Blooms*, 18.

34. Hirsh, *Bits and Pieces: Textile Traditions*, 46.

# BIBLIOGRAPHY

Adams County Quilt Project Committee. *The Hands That Made Them...: Quilts of Adams County, Pennsylvania.* Camp Hill, Pa.: Planks Suburban Press, 1993.

Brackman, Barbara. *Clues in the Calico.* McLean Va.: EPM Publications, Inc., 1989.

_____. *Encyclopedia of Applique.* McLean, Va.: EPM Publications, Inc., 1993.

_____. *Encyclopedia of Pieced Quilt Patterns.* Paducah, Ky.: American Quilters' Society, 1993.

_____. et al. *Kansas Quilts and Quilters.* Lawrence: University Press of Kansas, 1993.

Carlson, Linda Giesler. *Roots, Feathers and Blooms: 4-Block Quilts, Their History and Patterns, Book I.* Paducah, Ky.: American Quilters' Society, 1994.

*The Centennial Exhibition.* Rand McNally & Co., 1876.

Clark, Ricky. *Quilted Gardens: Floral Quilts of the 19th Century.* Nashville: Rutledge Hill Press, 1994.

_____ ed. *Quilts in Community: Ohio's Traditions.* Nashville: Rutledge Hill Press, 1991.

Fox, Sandi. *For Purpose and Pleasure: Quilting Together in Nineteenth-Century America.* Nashville: Rutledge Hill Press, 1995.

_____. *Small Endearments: Nineteenth-Century Quilts for Children and Dolls.* 2nd ed. Nashville: Rutledge Hill Press, 1994.

Granick, Eve Wheatcroft. *The Amish Quilt.* Intercourse, Pa.: Good Books, 1989.

Herr, Patricia T. *"The Ornamental Branches": Needlework and Arts from the Lititz Moravian Girls' School, between 1800 and 1865.* Virginia Beach: The Donning Company, 1996.

*Historical Review of Berks County.* 58, 1 (Winter 1992-1993).

*History of Beaver Meadows, Carbon County.* In commemoration of its Sesquicentennial, September, 1937.

Horton, Laurel, ed. *Quiltmaking in America: Beyond the Myths.* Nashville: Rutledge Hill Press, 1994.

Houck, Carter. *The Quilt Encyclopedia Illustrated.* New York: Harry N. Abrams, Inc., 1991.

*Illustrated Guide to Fairmount Park and the Centennial Exhibition.* Philadelphia: J.B. Lippincott & Co., 1876.

Johnson, Mary Elizabeth. *Star Quilts.* New York: Clarkson Potter Publishers, 1992.

Kimball, Jeana. *Red and Green: An Applique Tradition.* Bothell, Wash.: That Patchwork Place, Inc., 1990.

Kiracofe, Roderick. *The American Quilt: A History of Cloth and Comfort, 1750-1950.* New York: Clarkson Potter Publishers, 1993.

Lasansky, Jeannette. *Bits and Pieces: Textile Traditions.* Lewisburg, Pa.: Oral Traditions Project of the Union County Historical Society, 1991.

_____. *In the Heart of Pennsylvania: 19th and 20th Century Quiltmaking Traditions.* Lewisburg, Pa.: Oral Traditions Project of the Union County Historical Society, 1985.

_____. *In the Heart of Pennsylvania: Symposium Papers.* Lewisburg, Pa.: Oral Traditions Project of the Union County Historical Society, 1986.

_____. *On the Cutting Edge: Textile Collectors, Collections and Traditions.* Lewisburg, Pa.: Oral Traditions Project of the Union County Historical Society, 1994.

_____. *Pieced By Mother: Over 100 Years of Quiltmaking Traditions.* Lewisburg, Pa.: Oral Traditions Project of the Union County Historical Society, 1987.

_____. *Pieced By Mother: Symposium Papers.* Lewisburg, Pa.: Oral Traditions Project of the Union County Historical Society, 1988.

McMorris, Penny. *Crazy Quilts.* New York: E.P. Dutton & Co., Inc., 1984.

Montgomery, Florence M. *Textiles in America, 1650-1870.* New York: W. W. Norton and Company, 1984.

Nicoll, Jessica F. *Quilted for Friends: Delaware Valley Signature Quilts, 1840-1855.* Winterthur, Del.: The Henry Frances DuPont Winterthur Museum, 1986.

Orlofsky, Patsy and Myron. *Quilts in America.* New York: McGraw-Hill Book Company, 1974.

Roan, Nancy and Donald. *Lest I Shall Be Forgotten.* Green Lane, Pa.: Goschenhoppen Historians Inc., 1993.

Robinson, Robert L. *The Wickersham Letters, 1849-1887*, 1984.

Safford, Carleton L., and Robert Bishop. *America's Quilts and Coverlets.* New York: E.P. Dutton & Co., Inc., 1980.

Williams, Charlotte Allen. *Florida Quilts.* Gainesville: University Press of Florida, 1992.

(detail)
Catalogue 81.10